AF166041

Wolfgang Schnepper

Soccer Coaches: Perfect Training for Youth Soccer Players (5 to 10 years)

Wolfgang Schnepper, Born 1964, Cetified Sports Teacher
Ex-Bezirksliga player in football,
1988-89 successful german triathlete,
1990 Bayerischer champion in Body-Building,
1998 / 99 Fitness coach in paid football,
2003 - 2006 Physical education teacher at a comprehensive
school

Bibliografische Informationen der Deutschen
Nationalbibliothek: Die Deutsche Nationalbibliothek
verzeichnet diese Publikation in der Deutschen
Nationalbibliografie; detaillierte bibliografische Daten sind
im Internet über http://dnb.d-nb.de abrufbar.

Herstellung und Verlag: Books on Demand GmbH
Norderstedt
Satz und Layout: Wolfgang Schnepper

ISBN 978-3-7347-0108-5

Inhalt

Preface...6
Tactics in children`s football........................8
Tasks of a football coach for children................9
Training exercises...................................11
Race with gym mats...................................12
Station run..14
Shadow run...16
Engine on..16
Blind flea...17
Great white shark....................................17
The monkey game......................................19
Chain catching game..................................20
Catching tails.......................................21
Race...22
A piglet wants to be fed.............................24
Piglet wants to play football........................25
Pirate game..26
Fire-Water-Sandstorm.................................27
Supervisor...28
Stray eskomos..29
Who is afraid of the bad wolf?.......................29
A slightly mor difficult game........................30
Exercises only for the gym...........................30
Stand up, run up.....................................32
Catch the thieves....................................32
Children skittles....................................33
Piggy in the middle..................................34
Warm-up exercise / throwing exercise / dexterity.....35
Many dribbling, feinting and goal-shooting exercises
and bibliography..............................36 - 76

Preface

In this book we describe over 80 exercises for little footballers (5 to 10 years).

Rules of conduct and principles towards the little footballers are discussed first.

Coaches have a great responsibility towards the children. Never before have so many boys and girls of preschool age played football.

That`s why training for this age group must be fun for the first moment.

Contents and methods from the youth sector may not be adopted for the children, otherwise the number of football-playing children will shrink.

The first impressions of football training are crucial for the children. In case of incompetent behaviour of the trainer, parents or caretakers get little athletes a first negative impression. have bad experiences and in the worst case they develop an aversion to any football club.

Here we recognize the great importance of child-friendly behavior from coaches and caretakers.

Furthermore, the trainers need subject-specific knowledge and a high level of knowledge of human nature.

The footballing aspect must not be in the foreground for very young children.

The training refers to running, jumping throwing, ball games and games of various kinds. The fun factor and the community are in the foreground. The children need to feel that they are needed by the community. Every cild receives an equal amount of praise and recognition from trainers, parents and caretakers.

The trainer also has the important task of moderating very

ambitious parents.

The performance of the children is not yet so important.

Competitive games must have a great fun factor, mainly played and trained in small groups.

Children don`t just need footballs, pylons and slalom poles.

For a versatile development they need different balls, easy climbing course, playgrounds, swings and slides, gymns with balls and gym mats, foam balls for different games and much more.

This versatile sporting activity and the playing in groups is essential for the development of motor skills, training of social behaviour and empathy, prevention of postural weakness and to promote a sporting and human personality.

The exercises and games must not to be difficult for the small children. Otherwise the children tire to quickly.

The range of exercises is wide-ranging, must do without long explanation and always arouse the imagination and curiosity of the children.

Notice: Difficult technical exercises, the training of any tactics, long explanations and emerging boredom have no place in young children's football.

When the children play a football game and everyone always runs towards the ball, then let them.

Intuitively, they basically play modern football. Only moving them doesn`t work yet.

Adherence to fixed spaces is counterproducktive for the small footballers and contradicts modern football.

Of course, this does not mean that players should not take positions. Rather, it is about giving them as much freedom as possible.

In practice, this means that every player (e.g. a defender) should constantly paricipate in defense or attack.

It is enough to say to a defender: "If the opponent has the ball, please run backwards."

In addition, each child is allowed to try out all player positions.

 # Tasks of a football coach

Tasks of a football coach for children

- Only if the adults meet the children with openness and enthusiasm, the children feel comfortable and safe.

- The children are praised and motivated again and again.

- Positive qualities and values are exemplified.

- Fun and joy are conveyed und enthusiasm for football is exemplified.

- Poor performance of children is not criticized.

- Overly ambitious parents are moderated by the trainer friendly but decisive.

- Negative shouts from spectators and parents to the children, the referee, caretakers or coaches are to be avoided. Here, caretakers and trainers must intervene in a friendly manner.

- Coaches, supervisors and parents must cleverly bring children`s birthday parties into the training operation.

- Every child is treated with the same respect.

- Dangerous exercises are not used in children`s trainiing.
This means, for example: Dangerous climbing exercises, header with hard inflated leather balls, tacklings exercises, etc.

 # Tasks of a football coach

- A short meeting before a football match is perfectly sufficient.

- Every child is allowed to play long enough, never paying attention to the score or even tactics.

- The trainer always greets and says goodbye to the children within the whole group.

- The children are always cheered on and goals or substitutions be clapped.

- Every child is allowed to be a game leader.

- During the half-time break, the children are always offered drinks.

- The half-time speech is very short and the children are addressed personally and encouragingly.

- The children are praised for their strengths, but not addressed about their weknesses.

- Coaches in children`s football are predominantly comforters, mediators, jokers, educators and friends.

 # Training exercises

All described exercisis can be used at the age of 5 to 8 years. The selection depends on the physical performance level and cognitive abilities.

The duration of the exercises should not be determined in advance. If an exercise is fun for the children, the time frame is increased and vice versa.

As a rule, every training session ends with a real football match.

Between 4 to 6 years old, a training session last only 60 minutes. Between 7 to 8 years old a training session lasts 70 to 80 minutes.

Why should a training session for the little ones only last 60 minutes?

The little ones tire very quickly. The muscles are still awake and ths ability to concentrate is still very low.

At the first signs of fatigue in a child, this is cleverly spared in the further course of training.

Nor must we forget that children have a completely different sense of time. One hour of concentrated movement and play to the very little ones is comparable to a three-hour adult training.

At the beginning of each training session, it is advisable to give the children a free phase. In the first minutes of training they are allowed to move freely on the training field.

They can run with or without a ball, shoot or throw the ball. They can play in groups or occupy themselves alone.

In doing so, they break down excess energy and the ability to concentrate for further training increases.

Training exercises

Children do not yet need a warm-up program like adults and almost never injure themselves during normal loads.

In the following training sessions we refer to this section as the "free phase" which is usually 5 to 6 minutes.

Welcome Phase

After the free phase, the children are called and there is a short gathering. They will be greeted and the first exercise will be briefly explained.

Exercises almost without football-specific background

Race with gym mats

The exercise described here is intended exclusively for the gym.
Two groups are formed, in which the children stand one behind the other. A relay race will be conducted (see also the following picture).
The starting runners start running on the command of the coach. After a few meters, they must first run over one or two thin gym mats in the longitudinal direction.
Now follows a very thick soft mat.
Here the children jump on it, run over this mat and jump down and run again on a thin gym mat.
Then it is about a pylons and with a sprint back to the start.
Here the next child is clapped, which then also starts.
The team that finishes all runners first is, of course, the winner.

 # Training exercises

This exercise serves to train the feeling of movement (walking on different surfaces), stabilization of the joints and promotion of acceleration.

Variation of the exercise: After the children have run over the last mat, they run towards a handball goal.
A few meters in front of the goal, balls are next to each other, each one meter apart.
Before the runners run back, they have to shoot a ball into the goal. If they can do it, they can run right back.
If the goal shot fails, they havt to run to the goalpost, touch it and only then sprint back to the next starter.
The goal shot becomes more and more difficult with the last runners, because usually the balls are shot last, which are further out.

Further variation: Flagpoles are set up in front of the mats, which must first be passed through in the slalom.

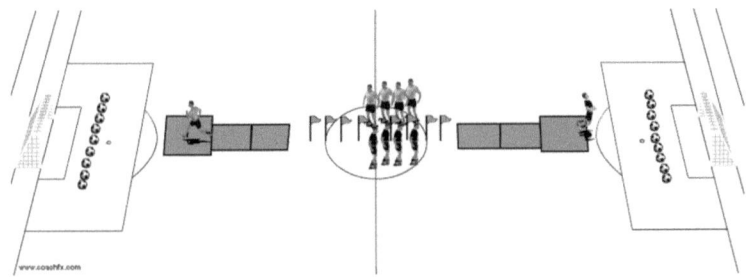

 # Training exercises

Station run

Here a field of about 15 by 15 meters is marked. Various stations are set up in this field, which each child should master once. Each station is set up twice, i.e. each station is carried out twice.

Examples for stations:

- Two jump ropes are stretched on thr hall floor. The children should balance safely on the rope from the beginning to the end of the rope.

- There are also two small balls in the field, for example, foam balls. These must be thrown vertically upwards once slightly over the head and then caught.

- Lay out two small gym mats and push them together with two boxes each so that they bend like a half-tube. Here the children should crawl through once.

- Place two times two small gym mats with the long side next to each other (see picture on the next side). The distance between is about 30 centimeters. Here the children should run through without touching the edges of the mat.

Training exercises

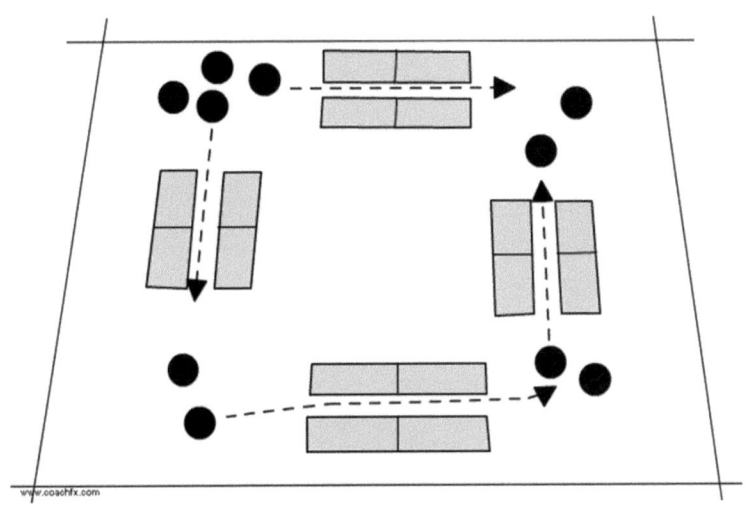

 # Training exercises

Shadow run

A square is staked out in which pairs are formed. Here, one is designated as a shadow giver and the other as a shadow.
The shadow giver runs off and performs various tasks, such as running backwards, jumping various spins, etc.
The shadow runs behind and imitates all movements of the shadow giver.Here, of course, it is advisable to repeat the exercise with ball.

Engine on

Small and large mats are laid out throughout the hall. Tunnels with gym mats and small gym boxes can also be formed again. With pylons and flagpoles small dribbling courses are created (see picture on the next page).
The cildren are now motorcycles, cars, buses or trucks. They should drive around the mats, through the tubes and slalom around the pylons and flagpoles. They should also make engine noises, honk their horns and pay attention to oncoming traffic. After this game, the whole thing is repeated with ball.

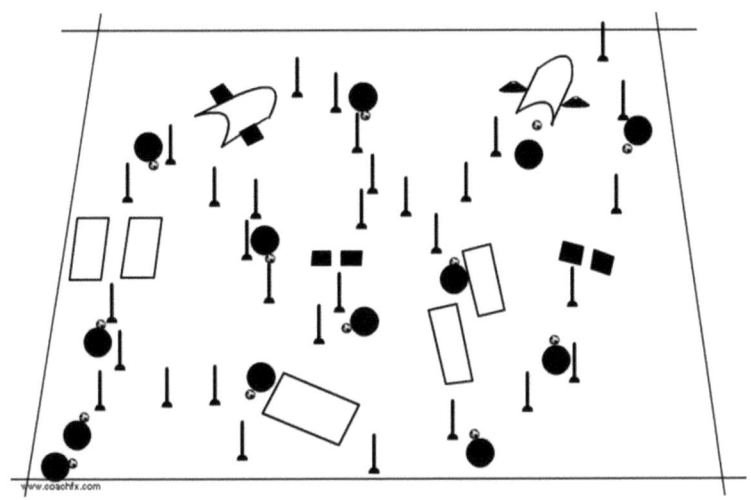

Blind flea

A square that is not too large is staked out. All children are
fleas and are allowed to move only by jumping. A player is
designated as a "blind flea" and gets blinfolded. The aim of
the blind flea is to catch another flea, the blind flea is allowed
to hop as often as it wants. The other fleas are allowed to
hop only 5 to 10 times in total. If a flea is caught, it becomes a
blind flea.

Training exercises

Great white shark

The children swim in the Atlantic Ocean (left square) and make swimming movements lying down.
The trainer shouts: "The shark is coming". Now all the children get up as quickly as possible and run to the rescue shore (right square).

Variation: Next to the swimming children there is a ball, which they have to lead into the other field during the warning call.

 # Training exercises

The monkey game

The next exercise, like the previous one, is suitable for the gym and the football field. The children are divided into two groups and line up as in the picture below.

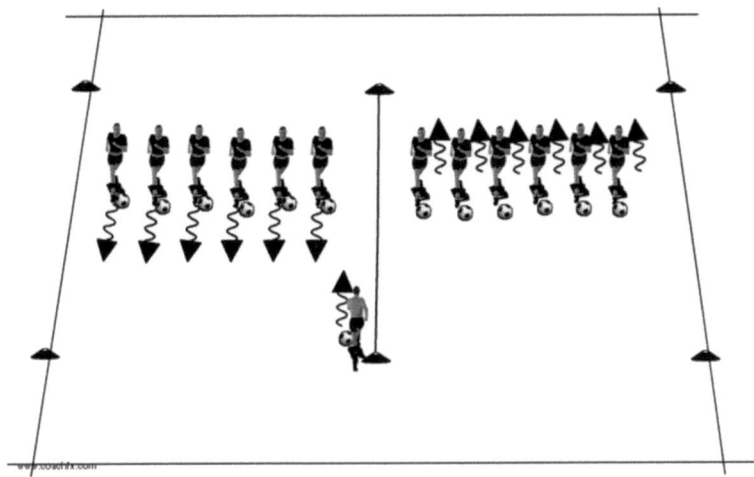

One group are chimpanzees who are very smart and want to annoy the trainer. The other group are the orang-utans, who are well-behaved and obedient. The trainer now demonstrates movements and the monkeys are supposed to imitate everything mirror-like. The orang-utans now imitate everything exactly, but the chimpanzees do exactly the opposite, because they want to annoy.

If the coach runs forward, the chimpanzees simply run backwards. Ih he jumps to the right, they also jump to the right, which is wrong in this case because it is mirror-inverted. If the coach circles the right arm, the chimpanzees also circle the

right arm, etc.

After some time, the tasks are exchanged. After this exercise, the same is done with one ball per child.

Chain catching game

The whole gym or outside a marked field is the playing field.

The players spread out on the playing field. The catcher tries to catch a player. If this succeeds, thre are two catchers who have to hold each other`s hand. So they have to catch next child. The chain gets bigger and bigger until the last child is caught.

Training exercises

Catching tails

The whole gym or outside a marked field is the playing field.

Each child is given a football shirt in the back of the waist-band. The children try to get as many shirts as possible and keep their own. The game is over when all shirts are caught. Who caught the most?

Training exercises

Race

The next exercise is a very nice exercise in relay form. It is very suitable for the gym and also the football field.

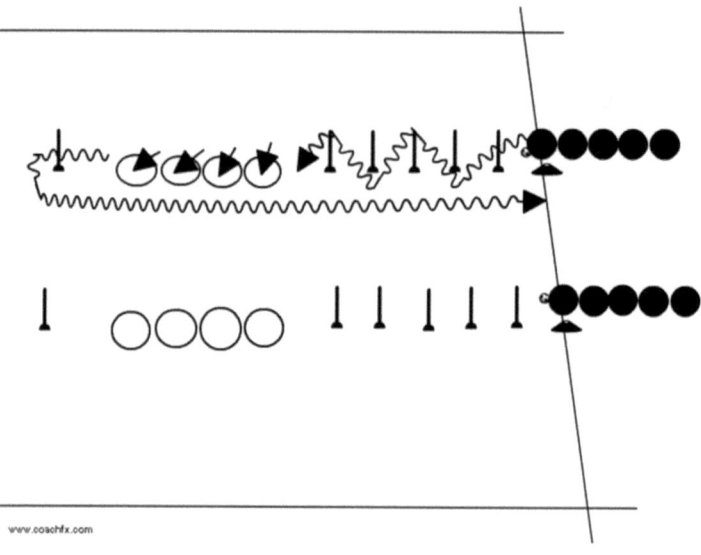

www.coachfx.com

Two groups are formed, which stand about five meters apart. The respective group members stand in a row. In front of each group, four to five pylons or flagpoles are set up in a row in a distance of one meter. After that, three to five gymastic tires are placed directly together in a row. A few meters behind it, a pylons or flagpole is paced again.

The starting runners of each group start at a signal: Slalom through the pylons or flagpoles, with a foot attachment in the gymnastic tires on to and around the last pylons and then with a full sprint directly back to the start.

Training exercises

Here the next runner is clapped and runs off with the same task. The group that has all the runners back at the finish line is of course the winner.

At the next round, the children must now carry a ball and hand it over to the next child in the finish area.

In the last competition, the level of difficulty is significantly increased again. Now the ball has to be dribbled through the flagpoles. then the ball is picked up and has to be bounced once into each gymnastics tire and caught again. After the last gymnastic tire, the ball is placed on the ground, guided around the last pylons or flagpole with the foot and then dribbled back to the next runner.

A piglet wants to be fed

www.coachfx.com

For this exercise we need four tablespoons and two potatoes that fit optimally into these spoons.

Which team feeds his piglet first?

Two teams stand next to each other and each five meters away from a flagpole. The starting runners run with their spoons in their hands and the potato in the spoon towards the flag, then around the flag and back to the start.
After they haved crossed the starting line again, the are allowed to take the potato in their hands and put it in the spoon of the next runner, who then starts running, etc.
The last runner must then run with the potato in the spoon to the piglet zone. Only here is allowed to take the potato in the hand and put it down to the piglet.

Training exercises

If a child loses the potato on the way, it must pick it up, put in the spoon again and only then continue running.

Piglet wants to play football

Now the same exercise is performed, but with a football. The first runners now hold a ball with both hands and run around the flagpole again and finally pass the ball to the next,etc. The last runner runs back to the piglet and gives him the ball. **Which team hands the ball to the piglet first?**

Piglet is shot

Each child gets a ball and everyone dribbles at the same time a goal in which the coach stands. From an agreed distance, all children shoot at the goal at the same time. No, they don`t want to score a goal. But who hits the "piglet" between the two posts?

Training exercises

Pirate game

All children play on a field with two goals in a team except for two pirates (see picture below but with two goals).

www.coachfx.com

Now there are many children who wear a shirt in the back of their pants. They are the merchant ships. Two children don`t wear a shirt, they are the pirate ships. They are enemy pirates, and their treasure chest here is there own football goal. The shirts of the merchant ships are expensive silk scarves. The pirates now try to steal the silk scarves and bring them into their treasure chest. The merchant ships, of course, try to escape.

# Training exercises

If a pirate has stolen an "expensive silk scarf", he must first bring it into his treasure chest before he can continue hunting. The winner is the pirate who has the most shirts in his treasure chest at the end and the "merchant ship" that keeps his goods on board until the end. This means that if the penultimate shirt is in the goal, the game is finished.

Of course, the same game is played afterwards with balls instead of shirts. The pirates will be exchanged. After that, a normal football game is a good idea.

Fire-Water-Sandstorm

Exercise structure and procedure:

The trainer calls the following commands.

- Water: All children must be on the benches.

- Sandstorm: Everyone lies down on the ground.

- Fire from there: All children have to run in the opposite direction to the end of the gym.

- Coffee gossip: Everyone sits down on the floor and clapping their hands.

 # Training exercises

Supervisor

This exercise is only suitable for children between three and six years of age. It can be played in the gym or on the football field.

First, a field of 20 by 20 Meters is marked. Two teams are formed, which move confused in the field. The children shall imagine that they are supervisors. After warming up the professional footballers, they have the task of collecting the balls as quickly as possible. That`s why there are balls on the field that are completely scattered and one ball per child. Each team also has a football goal.

The children now run all over the small football field. At the command of the coach, they should grab a ball with their hands as quickly as possible and get it into their goal.

After that, teh exercise is played a little differently. Now the children should dribble the ball into their goal as quickly as possible on command.

Which team is faster?

After these games, a normal football game is a good idea.

 # Training exercises

Stray Eskimos

The following two exercises are also only suitable for children between 3 and 6 years of age.

Four groups are formed. The children of two groups are the pilots and the others the Eskimos. Furthermore, two iglos are marked with pylons. The Eskimos are blindfolded and get lost. The pilots are allowed to guide the Eskimos to their iglo by acclamation.

Which group of pilots has their Eskimos fastest in the iglo?

Who is afraid of tha bad wolf?

Practice structure and procedure: One player is the wolf and the other players line up at the same height and in a row. The wolf stands a few meter behind the group. At some distance a square is marked, into which the players can escape.

The wolf asks: Who is afraid to the bad wolf?

Player: Nobody!

Wolf: And when he comes?

Player: Then we run!

All players then run off and the wolf tries to catch as many players as possible. But only a single touch is enough.

 # Training exercises

A slightly more difficult game

A field of 20 x 20 meters is marked with two football goals.
Two teams are formed, which als wear different football jer-
seys. The coach gives the two teams important names such as
Manchester City and FC Bayern München. The children are
told that they will meet in the final of the Champions-League.
In the marked field, both teams should now warm up.
Thie is done first without a ball and then with balls in groups
of two.
This is done first without a ball and then with balls in groups
of two. After this warm-up, of course, the longed-for endga-
me takes place. The playing time is 2 x 10 minutes.
In the event of a draw follows immediately a penalty shoot-
out.

Exercises only for the gym

- Two Teams are formed and a balloon competition is started.
Each child receives a balloon. The first child of each team runs
off with a balloon and has to place it in a large container.
Then both run back and clap off the next runner, who should
then also transport the balloon into the container. Each team
must carry the same number of balloons into the container.
Of course, the team that does this first wins.

Training exercises

- Each team (each team has its own zone) has two to three balloons per child in a certain zone. On command, all children of both teams should simultaneously push a balloon out of this zone into another marked zone with their feet (each team has its own zone here as well). Anyone who has managed this runs back and takes on the next balloon. The first team to transport all the balloons to the new zone wins. If a balloon bursts, the respective child gets a reserve balloon from the trainer, but has to start again in the original zone.

- Many pre-inflated balloons are placed in a marked field. The children should now shoot the balloons out of this area. When all the balloons have been shot out of the field, they are given the task of bursting the balls with the foot. The child picks up the leftovers. Whoever has collected the most leftovers wins the game.

Training exercises

Stand up, run up

Exercise structure and procedure: One child is selected as the catcher. The other children are in a fenced-off playing field. The catcher tries to catch the other children. If successful, the captive child must stop and straddle the legs. An uncaught child can free a captive child by crawling through the legs. The aim of the catcher is to catch as many other children as possible before a free child can free a trapped child. As a rule, it is advisable to use two or three catchers.

Catch the thieves

 # Training exercises

Exercise structure and procedure: Two or three children are selected as police officers. These kids get some kind of uniform. The remaining children are thieves. A prison is marked with four pylons. At the trainer's command, the police officers try to catch the thieves. Here a light touch is enough and the thief has to go to jail. Can the cops arrest all the thieves in a given time?

Children skittles

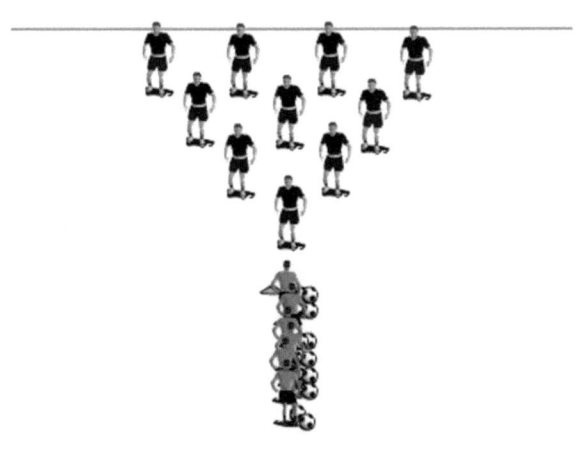

Two teams are formed again. The team to be bowled stands rigidly in the bowling room. The children have the idea that they are real skittles and are positioned accordingly (see picture above). The bowling team stands two meters away from the first cone at a marking that must not be crossed. Each bowler has two balls and rolls them onto the skittle one by one.

If a child is hit by a ball, it falls to the ground. Which team hits the most skittles?

Variation: Now the balls have to be shot.

Piggy in the middle

www.coachfx.com

In a relatively small playing field there is a catcher and always a child who has to be caught. The other children sit in groups of two close together and evenly spaced around the room. If the child being chased sits down in a group of two at the edge in time, so that three children are now sitting side by side, the child on the other side has to get up in time and run away because it has to take the position of the child being chased.

# Training exercises

If the hunted child is touched by the hunter, it becomes the hunter. The other child sits in a group of two and determines the next prey on the other outside.

Variation: The game starts with two hunters and two hunted.

Warm-up exercise / throwing exercise / dexterity

We will need 3 to 5 foam balls at least the size of a tennis ball. In a limited playing field, the children try to throw each other off. With the ball in your hand you can run a maximum of five steps and then you have to throw quickly. Children who are hit leave the playing area and now, together with the trainer, they have the task of returning the balls that have been thrown out of the playing area. Thrown balls are picked up as quickly as possible and another attempt is made to throw someone. The last two or three children are winners. The exercise is usually repeated two or three times.

Many dribbling, feinting and goal-shooting exercises are following now:

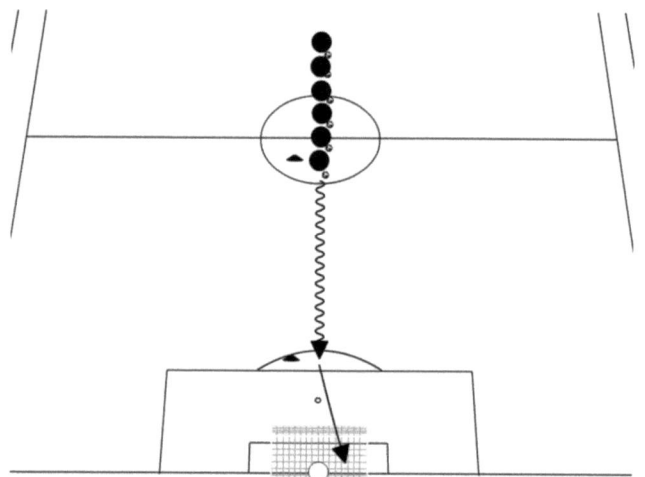

A playing field of 20 x 20 meters is marked with two soccer goals (see picture above, however, with one goal slightly offset on the other side).

Several children are standing in a row on the right-hand goal line of both goals, each with a ball. The first child dribbles towards the opposite goal and shoots at the goal from a distance of 7 to 15 meters. The distance depends on age and shot power. After that, the children retrieve their ball and line up again on the opposite side.

After a few minutes, this exercise is declared a competition: Which child will be the first to score five goals?

Training exercises

Dribbling and scoring practice for the gym

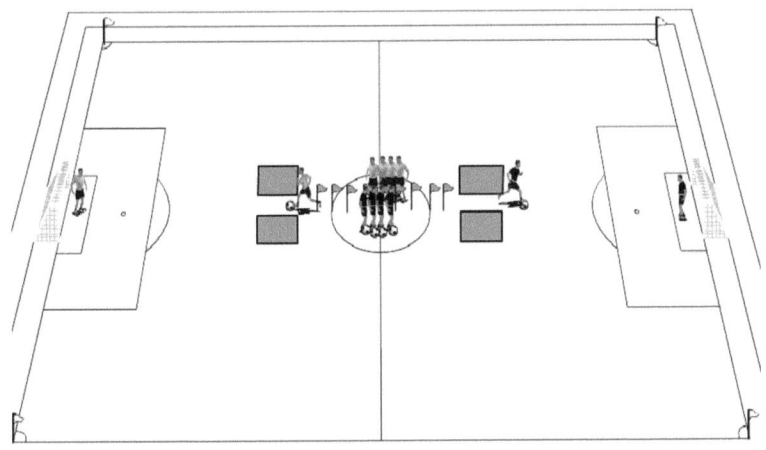

Each team chooses a goalkeeper who can be changed at will. The children run with the ball, dribble through the flagpoles, skilfully lead the ball through the gymnastics mat channel and shoot at the soccer goal. Now the next child is running. The starting runners line up at the back.

Training exercises

Hütchenwald

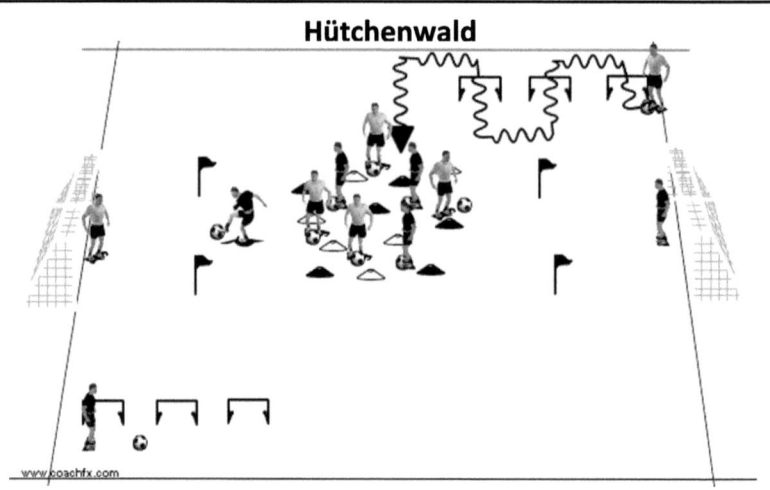

Training exercises

Exercise structure and procedure: The children are divided into two groups. Set up two goals with goalkeepers about 30 meters apart. Build cone forest with two different colors. Three small hurdles are set up next to the goals. Each group is assigned a goal and a forest of pylons. The children dribble in the cone forest and first have to touch four pylons of their own team with their hands while dribbling. The player then dribbles to the opposing goal and shoots from a marked line at the goal. On the way back to the cone forest, they dribble to the hurdles. The ball is played through the hurdles and the player jumps over them (see picture on the last page).

Variation: Take the ball in your hands in front of the pylons and jump over the pylons.

Two occupied goals next to each other

There are now two occupied goals next to each other. At a distance of about 25 meters, two groups stand in front of the own goal. Each player has a ball. There are two pylons in a row in front of the goals, the distance between them is about 4 to 5 meters.

Procedure: The first players in each group dribble around the first pylon, back to the start, then to the front pylon and finish there with a shot on goal. After the shot on goal, the next child starts. The shooting distance is of course adjusted to the power of the shot. The scorers get the ball, of course, and get back in line with their group.

39

Training exercises

Variation: The exercise is repeated on mini soccer goals without a goalkeeper and a competition is started. The players should now shoot the ball into the soccer goal from a distance of about 7 to 10 meters. If a child manages to do this, they have achieved their goal and are no longer in the competition.

If the shot on goal fails, the goal scorer must get his ball and join the group again. But you have to make sure that the next child only dribbles when their predecessor has shot.

Which group shot all the balls into the small soccer goal first?

Motor race

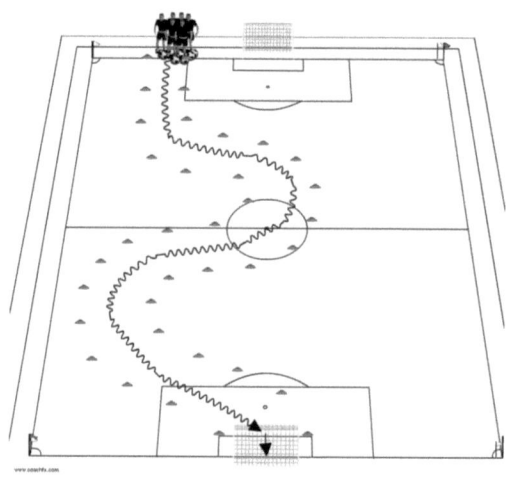

Structure of the exercise and procedure: A racetrack with pylons is set up, which leads to a soccer goal at the end (see picture above).

 # Training exercises

All children line up at the starting line with a ball. The race begins at the command of the trainer. The children dribble along the race track and shoot the ball into the soccer goal at the end of the track. Which kid will score the first goal? Variation: The children carry the ball and then put it in the goal at the end of the race track.

Dribbling competition for the gym

Two teams are formed. Within the teams, the children stand one behind the other, the starting runner is in possession of the ball. The groups stand about 10 meters apart. 20 meters in front of each group there is a large gym box with the wide side facing the children. There is a non-intrusive marking five meters in front of each box.

Procedure: When the starting command is given, the starting runners dribble in the direction of the box. At the height of the marking, they shoot the ball vigorously against it. the rebounding ball is accepted, dribbled back, and passed to the next child. The team that finishes all players first is of course the winner.

Target shooting

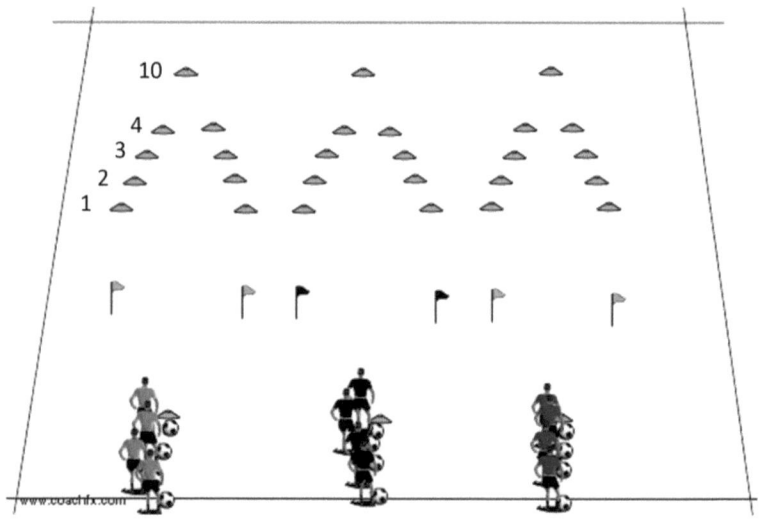

Exercise structure and procedure: Depending on the number of children and the trainer, three or more point fields (triangles) with pylons are set up. Behind them, for example, there is a slightly larger pylon. A shooting line is marked out with flagpoles about five meters in front of it (see picture above). At the coach's command, the first players in each group dribble to the shooting line and try to shoot through the scoring field from there.

For example, if the ball leaves the triangle after the third pylon, the player and his team get three points. The child gets his ball and quickly runs back to his group. Now the coach gives another command and it is the turn of the next child, etc. Which team has the most points after a few rounds?

Training exercises

Exercise of diversity

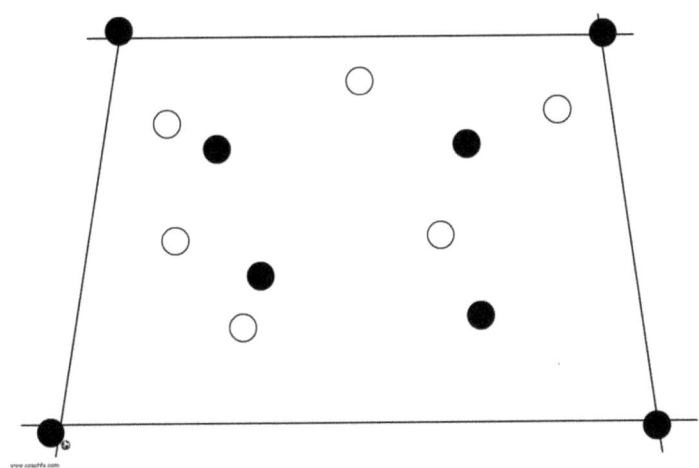

The first part of the exercise is performed without the ball. A field of 20 x 20 meters is marked. The children spread out in the field and run around freely. At the command of the trainer, they should briefly complete the following exercises, for example:

- Spider walk on all fours
- Roll sideways
- Crawl on all fours
- Hop on one leg
- Hop on both legs
- Hop run
- Two leg squat jump
- Skipping
- Knee-lever run

43

Training exercises

Next exercise: Now each child gets a ball. They dribble in this field with this ball. They are given a command to perform a specific football trick.

Line Dribbling

Exercise structure and procedure see upper picture

The light players try to defend their line. The dark players try to dribble through both lines. If this succeeds, there are two points. If only a line is dribbled, there is one point, if no line is dribbled, there is no point. After a specified time, the tasks are changed. Which team gets the most points?

44

 # Training exercises

Pylon soccer goal and partner game

www.coachfx.com

Exercise structure and procedure see upper picture

Pairs are formed, each with a ball. The child with the ball dribbles to the next pylon soccer goal and passes the ball through the pylon goal to the child who has run along. That child now dribbles to the next goal and passes the ball back through the goal to their teammate, and so on.

45

Two goalkeepers

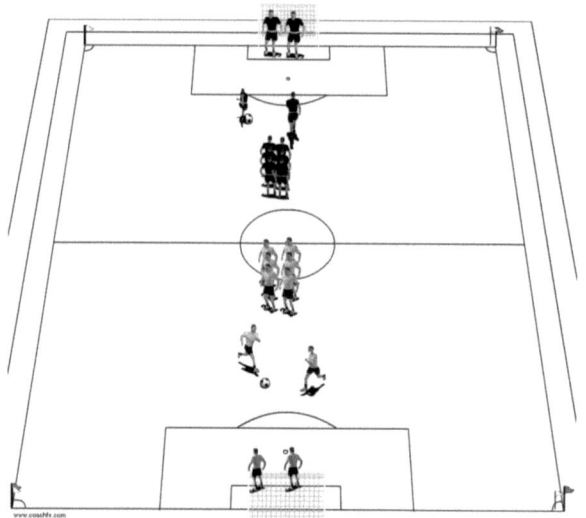

In this game, only groups of two are formed. A group of two are declared "invincible" goalkeepers and stand in the goal. The other groups of two run towards the goalkeeper one after the other with a ball and have to shoot at the soccer goal from a certain distance. During the dribbling, the ball also played to each other and the goal scorer is determined. If the shot on goal is successful, the groups of two swap roles and the goal scorers become goalkeepers.

Training exercises

Goal shot training under pressure

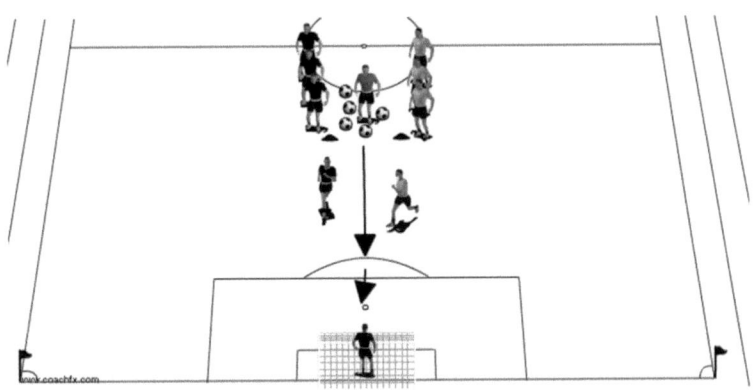

The children stand about 30 meters in front of the soccer goal in two groups behind each other (see picture above).
A goalkeeper is in the soccer goal. The trainer stands between the groups with a few balls and shoots a ball as straight as possible in the direction of the soccer goal with the appropriate speed of the ball. The first two children in each group now fight for the ball and for the goal. Then they bring the ball back to the coach and line up at the back. If there are many children, a second soccer goal with a goalkeeper is used.

Two pylons are set up offset about 30 meters in front of the goal and two groups are formed again (see picture above). At the command of the trainer, the first two children in each group start. The white player with the ball is looking for the goal, the black player tries to prevent him or even shoot at the soccer goal himself.

Training exercises

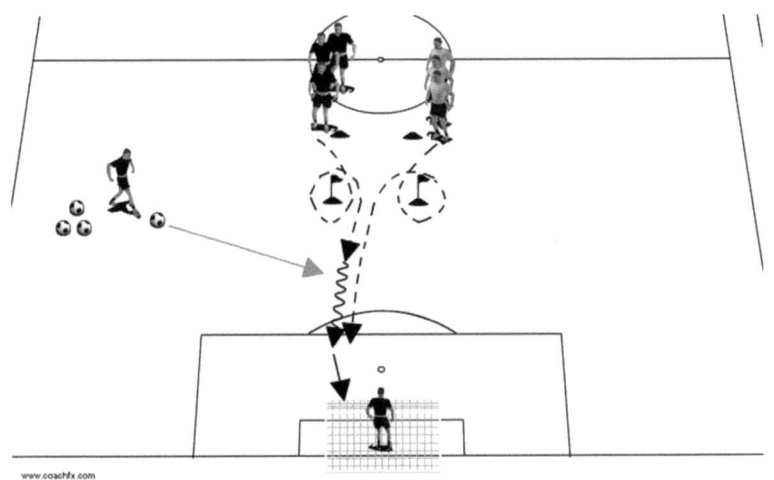

www.coachfx.com

The first two children start at the trainer's command, run around the flags and fight for the ball and the corresponding goal shot.

Training exercises

Exercise for training the inside instep

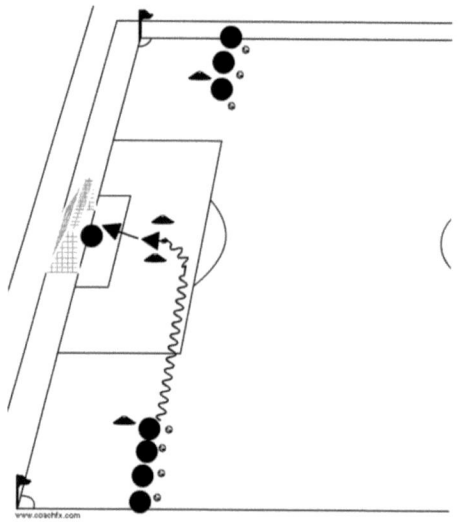

In this exercise, the children run parallel to the outer line of the goal from the side (see picture above). The distance to the soccer goal must be adapted to the age and level of performance. One group runs from the left and shoots with the right foot accordingly, the other group runs from the right and shoots with the left foot. The two sides take turns scoring the goal. After some time, the sides are completely changed.

Training exercises

Dynamic goal shooting exercise

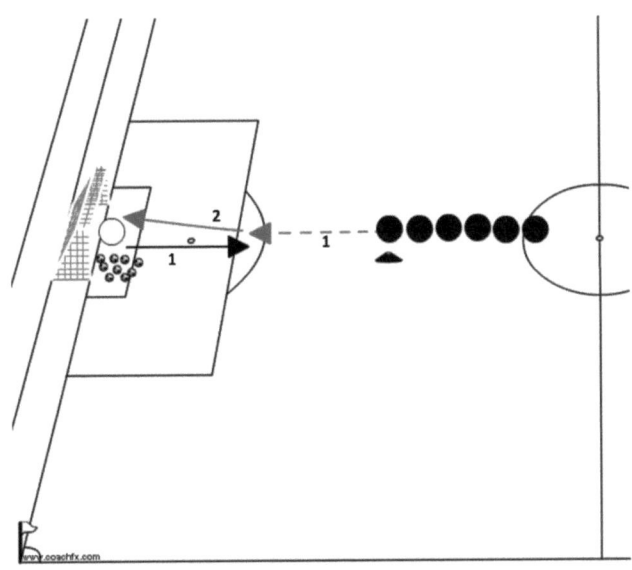

The coach is standing in the soccer goal with a lot of balls. The children stand in a row 20 meters centrally in front of the football goal (see picture above). The coach shoots the ball slightly towards the first goal scorer so that he catches the ball about 10-15 meters from the goal. The little soccer player runs towards the ball and is supposed to shoot it at the coach with full force and full instep. The coach tries to dodge and shoots a ball at the next scorer. After a few rounds, the children should shoot directly into the soccer goal.

Training exercises

Passing exercise for training with the inside of the foot

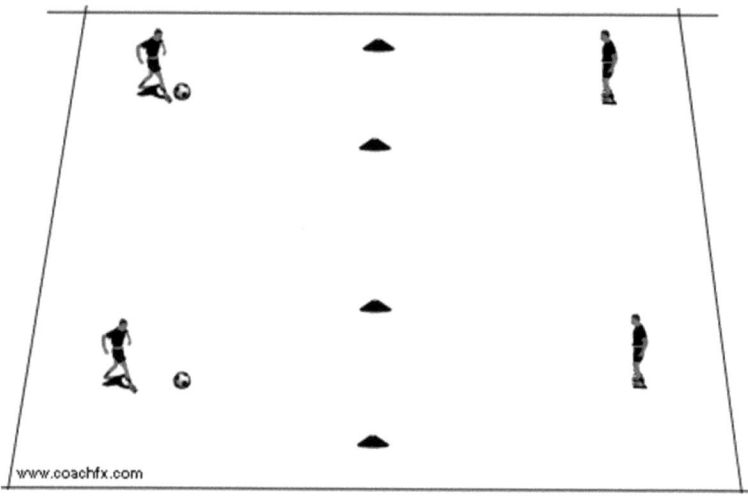

www.coachfx.com

The children take turns passing the ball with their left and right feet. It is only shot with the inside of the foot. The ball is first stopped and later played directly. The ball must always be played through two pylons.

Synchronized soccer goal shooting

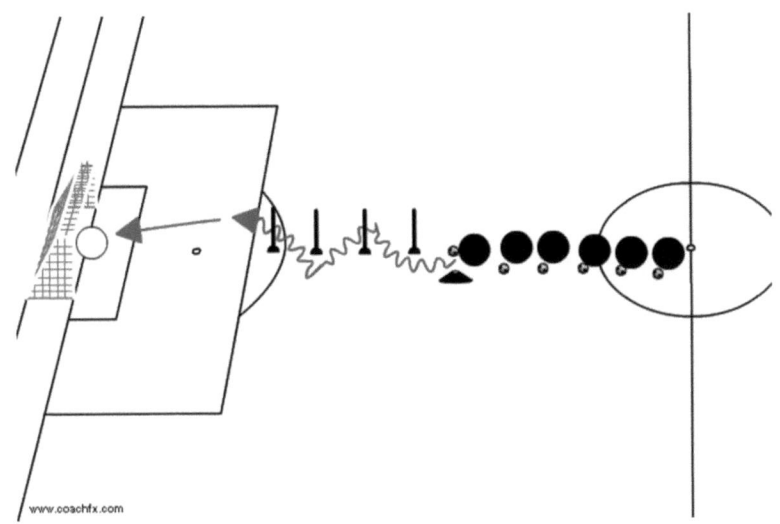

www.coachfx.com

Exercise structure and procedure: Two teams are formed.
The players stand one behind the other about 20 meters in
front of a youth goal, which is staffed by a coach. Every player
has possession of the ball. Almost directly in front of the
starting runner of each team there are four pylons in a row
one behind the other (see upper picture, however with two
groups two rows of pylons are intended). The distance
between the pylons is about one meter. The teams are about
five meters away from each other. After a command from the
trainer, the first child in each group starts running, slaloms
the ball through the pylons and ends the action with a shot
on goal. The trainer tries to hold the ball, which of course is
very difficult with synchronized shots.

Training exercises

Children who hit the goal end the game, everyone else has to queue up for their team. The first team to score all balls is the winner.
Game variants: The shooting technique or the kicking leg is awarded.

More dribbling competitions and goal-shooting exercises

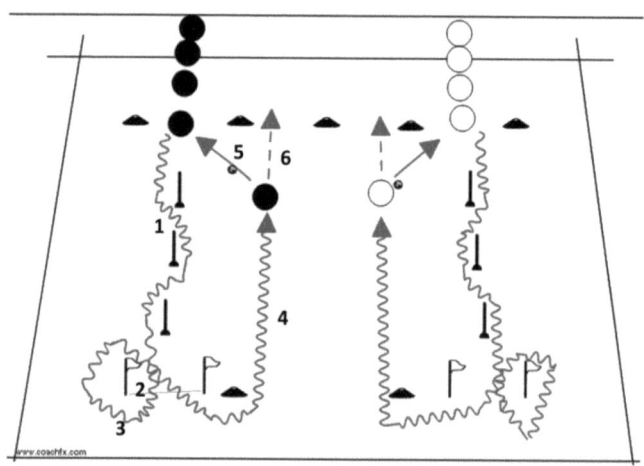

Two teams are formed (see picture above). At the trainer's command, the first two children start running with the ball and dribble through the pylons. Then the children go through the inside of the goal (white flags), walk around the chosen flag, run around the outside of the pylons and can now dribble back or pass. In the case of an inaccurate play, time can pass here. The team. who gets their last player with the ball over the starting line is of course the winner.

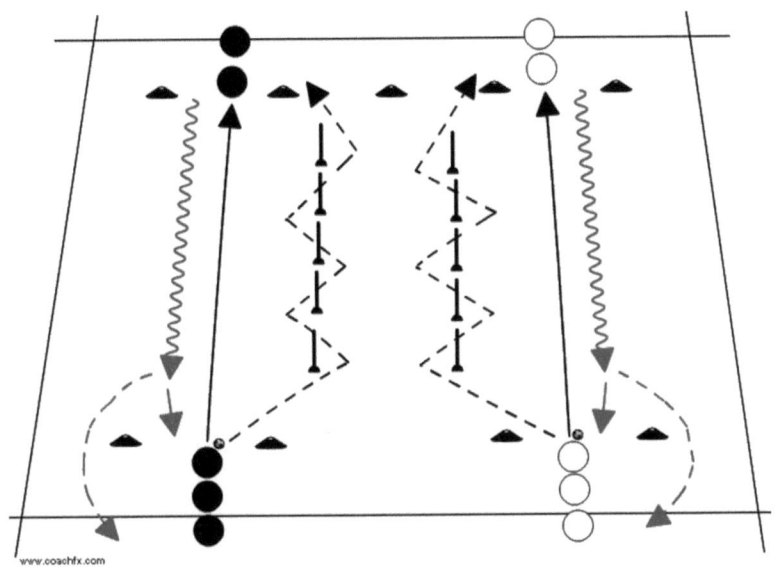

In this exercise, soccer player A passes soccer player B, who dribbles to soccer player A's position and hands the ball to the next player, lining up at the back. Player A runs through the flagpoles in the slalom at maximum speed and queues on the other side, etc. (see picture above).

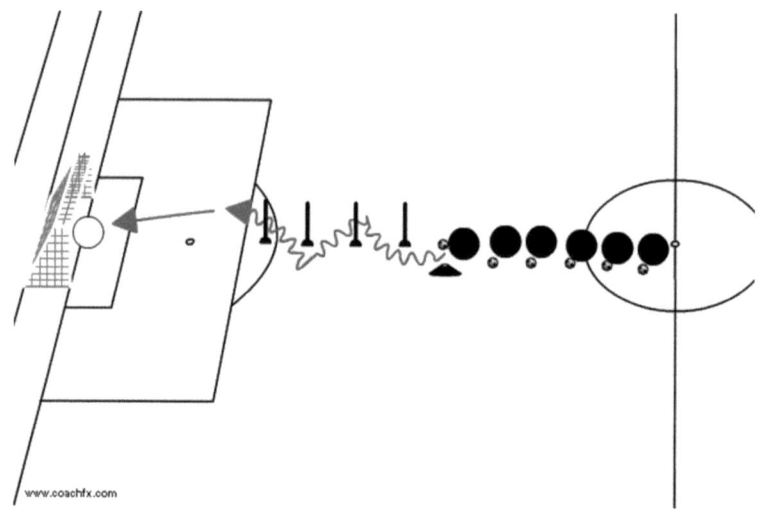

www.coachfx.com

In the next exercise, the children stand one behind the other with the ball in a row about 25 meters from the center of the goal. The first child starts running with the ball, dribbles through the flagpoles that are set up one behind the other and finishes with a shot at goal from 10 to 15 meters. The child takes his ball again and joins the row at the back.

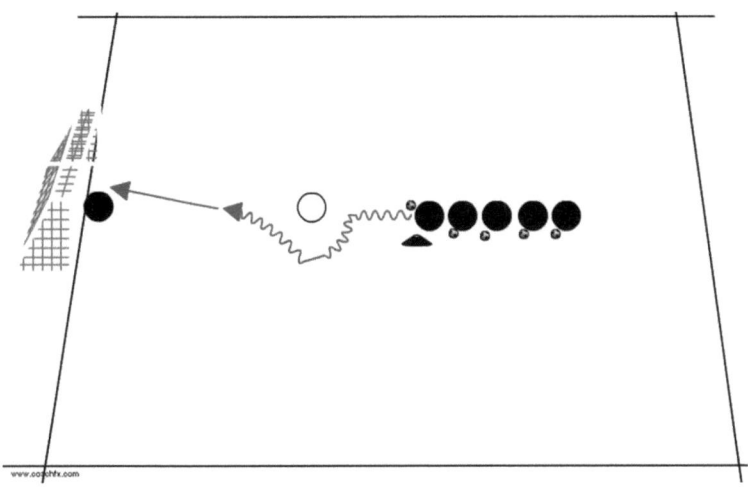

A soccer goal is staffed out by a goalkeeper, the coach positions himself about 15 meters centrally in front of the soccer goal, 10 meters further in front of it the children stand in a row (see picture above). The children run up to the trainer one after the other, practice a feint, pass the trainer and then look for the goal. However, the trainer only works lightly.

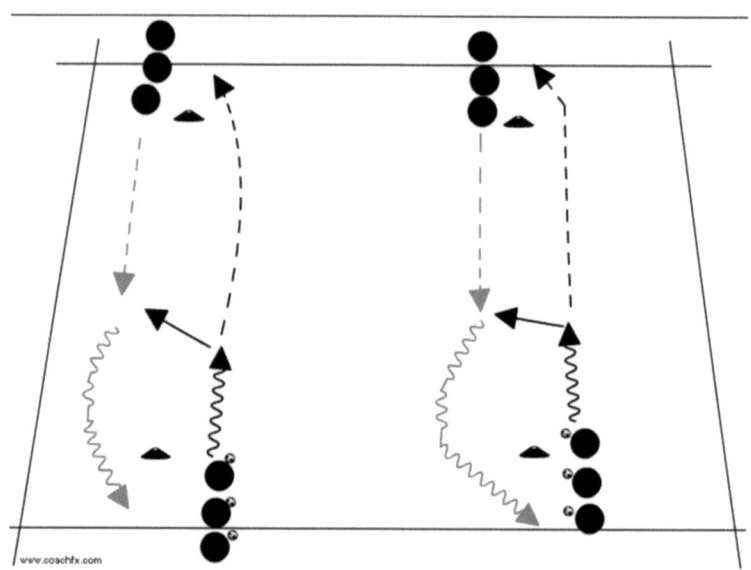

Exercise series for receiving the ball and passing the ball

Two pylons are set up at a distance of about 20 meters. Three children are standing one behind the other at each pylon, each child has a ball on one side (see picture above). At the trainer's command, the first children with the ball start with a speed dribbling in the direction of the other pylons. At the same time, the first children start towards the other side. If a distance of two to three meters is reached, a short pass is made to the other player. He now dribbles on to the other pylon and queues up there again. Now the next children start etc.

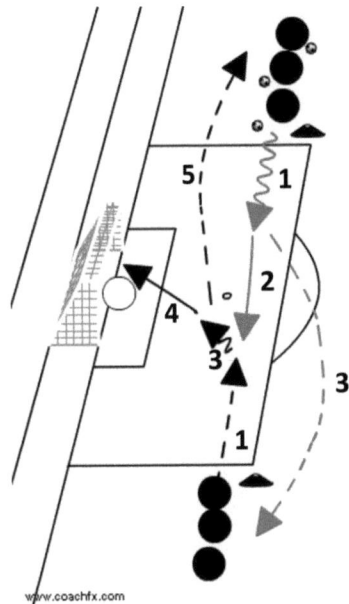

Then the same exercise takes place about 15 meters in front of a soccer goal. The children run towards each other parallel to the goal line. The player taking possession of the ball then finishes with a shot on goal from a goal distance of about 12 metres.

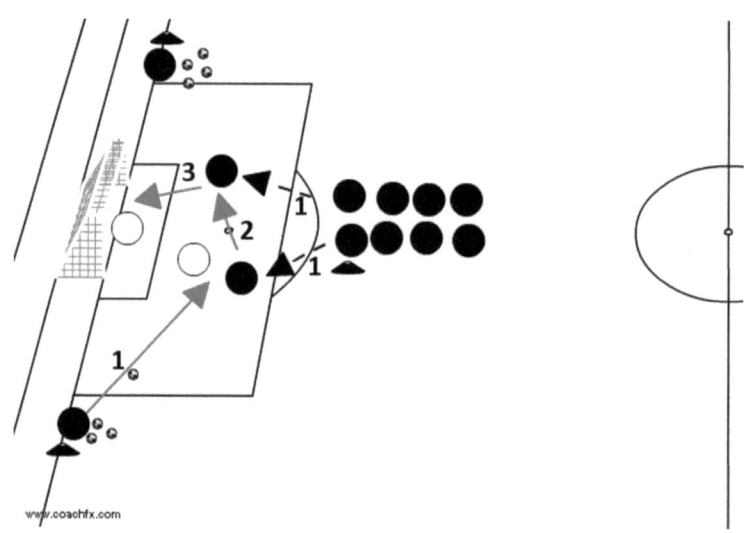

www.coachfx.com

Corner kick practice

The two crossers stand with their balls far away from the goal on the outer line of the goal, appropriate to their age, and alternately bring in corner balls. A player stands in the soccer goal and a defender supports him. The children stand in groups of two behind each other 20 meters in front of the soccer goal (see picture above). If they run towards the soccer goal together, a cross occurs from the left or right. The two attackers should now somehow achieve a goal. The defender and the goalkeeper should prevent them from doing so. After this action, the next two strikers start and the previous strikers line up at the back of the line. After some time, the positions are exchanged again and again.

We come to a playful training session that, among other things, is an excellent way of training soccer-specific endurance. First, a game is played on four small soccer goals without a goalkeeper. The field is kept relatively small. So the children have to keep moving, constantly switching from attack to defense and from defense to attack. Fast playing or short, fast dribbles with feints are enforced. Due to the high load, the playing time is limited to a maximum of 10 minutes. Then the game is played on four normal football goals, each with a goalkeeper.

Variation: It is played with two balls. Now more ball contacts and more fun are guaranteed.

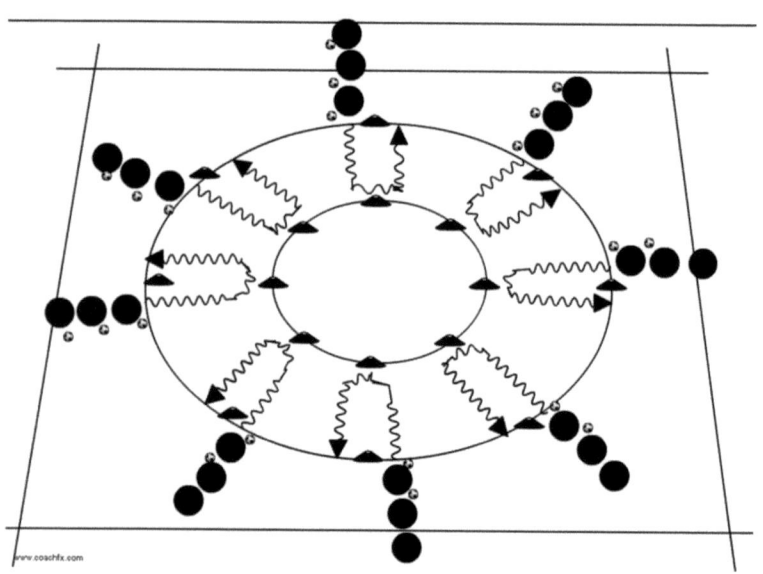

Dribble training

Three children stand one behind the other (see picture above), the front child is in possession of the ball and stands next to a pylon. Eight meters in front of the first child there is another pylon. The first child in each group dribbles to the front pylon at the coach's command, pulls the ball back with the sole and dribbles back to the first pylon. Here the ball is passed and the next child starts. Several passes are carried out one after the other. This is followed by a variation of the exercise. The children should turn completely around the pylons with tight ball control. The exercises are practiced alternately with the left or right foot.

Training exercises

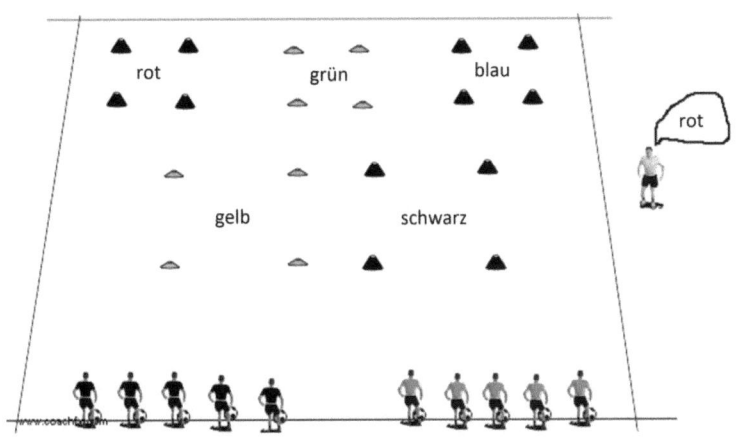

rot = red   grün = green   blau = blue   gelb = yellow
schwarz = black

Color dribbling

Structure of the exercise and procedure: A few colored squares with pylons are set up (see picture above). Two or more teams are formed. Each child receives a ball. The coach calls out a color and all children dribble into the appropriate square. If there are three teams, the first team to get all the children in the square first gets three points. The second team gets two points and the third team gets one point. Which team has the most points after five rounds?

Variation: The exercise takes place without the ball as a pure running competition.

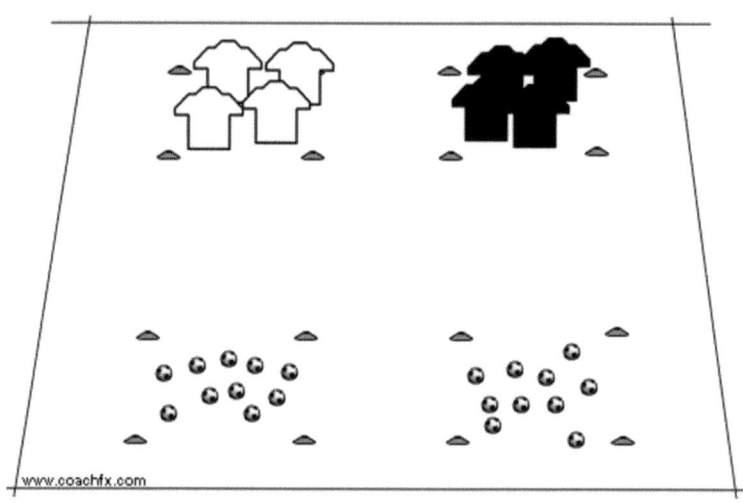

www.coachfx.com

Sprint competition

Four squares are formed and marked with four pylons each. The trainer forms two teams, which line up next to each other in a square (see picture above). In the other two squares, all balls are placed evenly distributed. At the trainer's command, the first players in each team start to their square and fetch a ball, which they carry with their hands. Which team will have all the balls in their square first?

Variation: The balls must be dribbled with the feet.

Training exercises

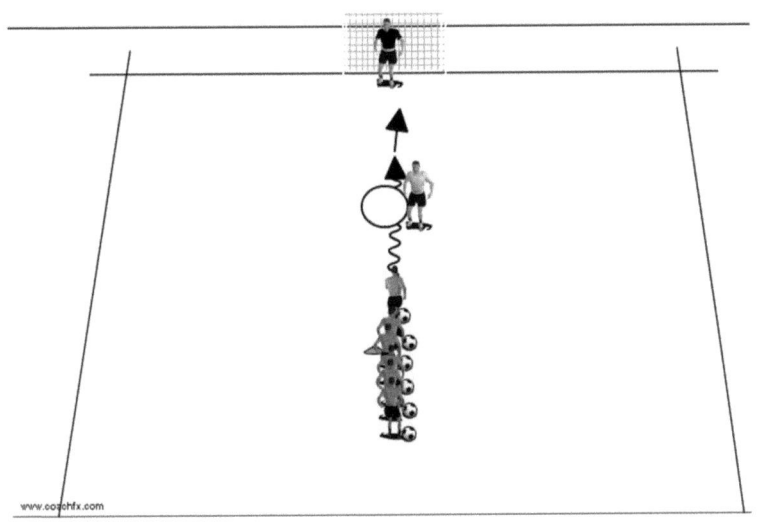

www.coachfx.com

Games, fun and excitement

The coach stands about 12 meters with a gymnastic hoop in front of a goal with a goalkeeper. The gymnastic hoop has ground contact with the lower edge. The children stand in a row about 20 meters in front of the goal, each with a ball (see picture above). The first child runs, shoots the ball easily through the gymnastic hoop and now has to crawl through the hoop himself. Then get up immediately and look for the soccer goal. Then the next child runs with the ball.

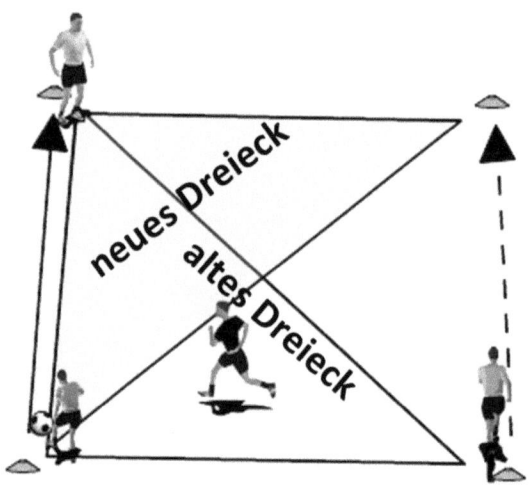

www.coachfx.com

3 against 1

A square with four pylons is marked (see picture above). Three children each occupy a pylon and are in possession of a ball. The opponent in the square tries to get the ball. One touch of the ball is enough. Then the positions are changed accordingly. Shooting the ball through the center of the square should be avoided. That is why the children at the pylons have to keep running to another pylon. Here the little soccer players learn the optimal movement within a soccer game with short play.

Training exercises

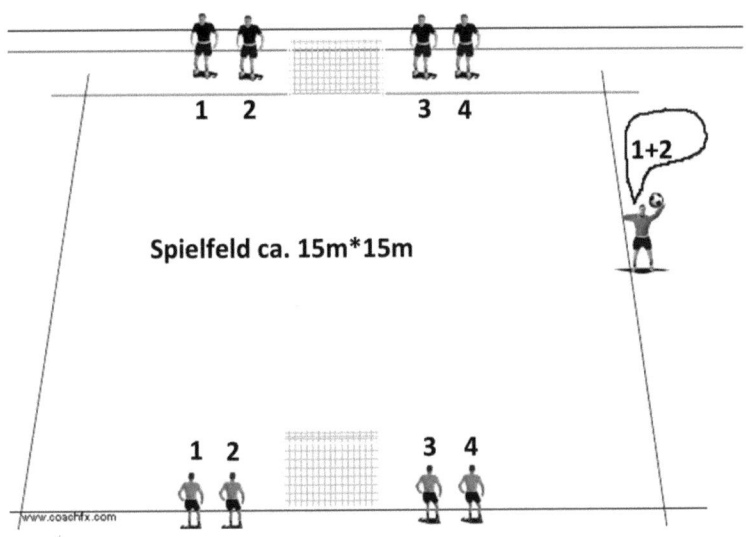

Spielfeld ca. 15m*15m

Matchfield: 15 meters x 15 meters

Training of football-specific endurance

Exercise structure and procedure see upper picture

Two teams are formed, each standing to the right and left of their soccer goal. Each player is given a number. The coach calls out a number or two and throws a ball into the field. The called children start on the field and try to score a goal. After a minute or two, new numbers are called and the players change. Variation: Now the game is played with fixed goalkeepers.

Training exercises

Technique training 1

Exercise structure and procedure see upper picture

Two pylons are set up at a distance of about 15 meters and occupied by players. The first child with the ball dribbles a few meters and then plays to the child on the other pylon. The b runs further through to the other pylon. The child who is being played runs towards the other player beforehand, dribbles around the front pylon and dribbles on to the other pylon. Now the child shoots on the next player and so on.

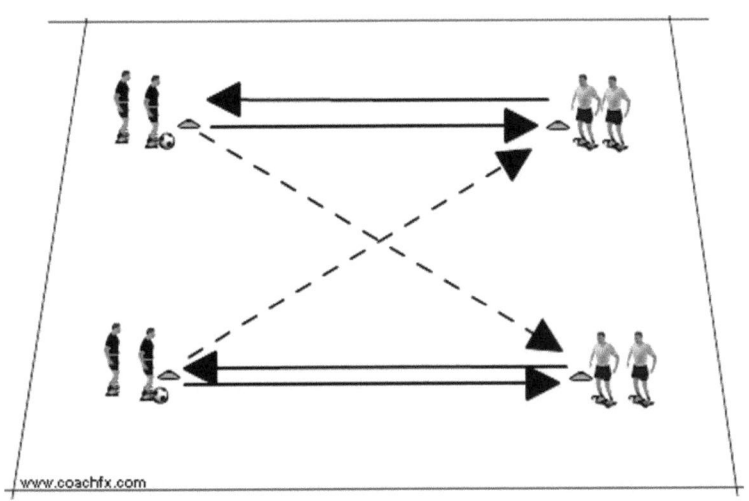

www.coachfx.com

Technique training 2

Exercise structure and procedure see upper picture

There are four groups facing each other, the two groups on one side each have a ball at the beginning. The two children with the ball shoot the ball to the child on the opposite side and then run diagonally to the other group.
Here they wait for the next ball, etc.

www.coachfx.com

Dribbling competition 1

Exercise structure and procedure see upper picture

Several teams are formed. Each team has a ball. At the command of the trainer, the first players in each team start and dribble through the slalom course. The ball may be shot back or dribbled straight back from the last pylon. Which team finishes first?

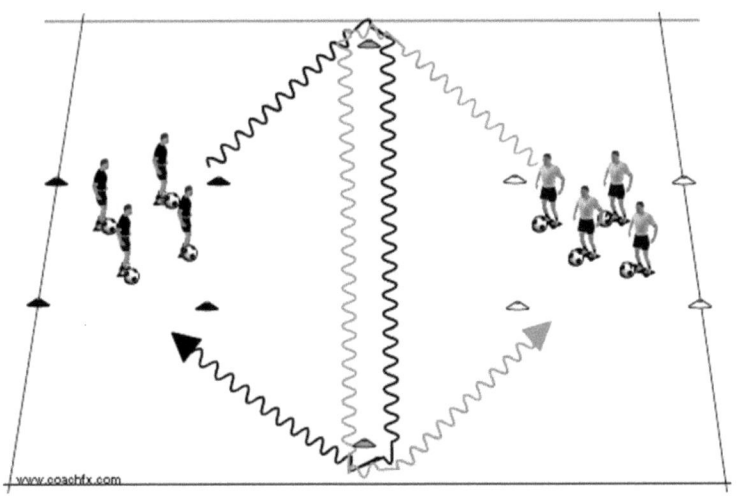

www.coachfx.com

Dribble competition 2

Exercise structure and procedure see upper picture

Two teams are formed. Each player gets a ball and a number. With eight children, for example, the numbers one to four are distributed in each team. The trainer now calls out a number, whereupon the respective children start and dribble through the course as in the picture above. The team whose child is back in their own square first gets a point. Multiple numbers can also be called. Which team has the most points after ten calls, for example?

71

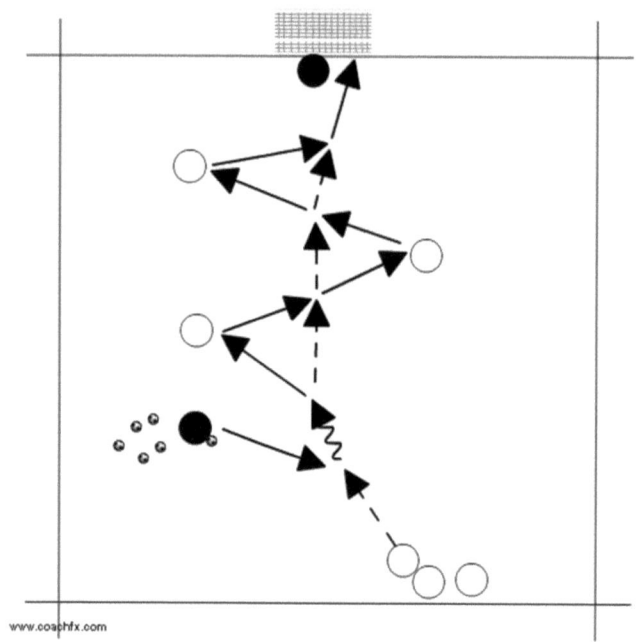

www.coachfx.com

Goal shot exercise

A player who has all of the balls, shoots the ball to a child in the opposite row (see picture above). This child takes the ball and dribbles to a teammate's first station and plays a one-two with him. This is then also done with the next station, etc. After the last one-two, the action ends with a shot on goal. The different positions are exchanged again and again. Many rounds are performed. The goal shot distance is adjusted to the age.

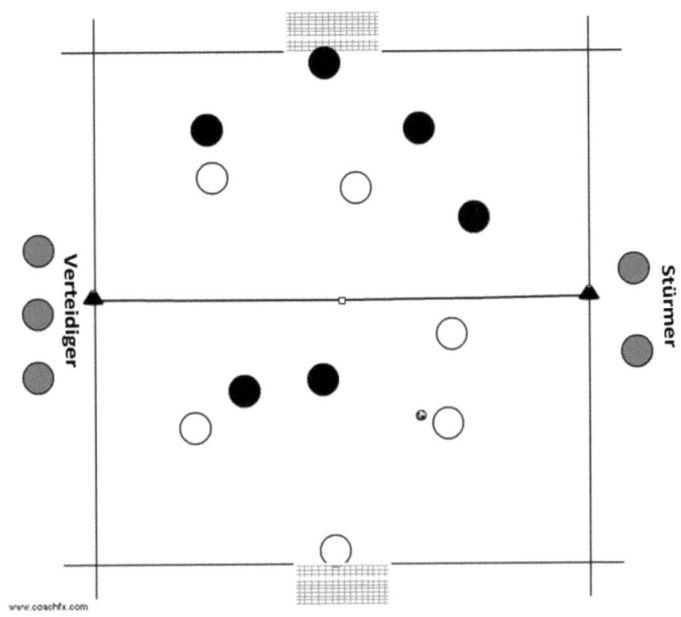

Outnumbered situation

Exercise structure: see picture above

Procedure: It is played on a small soccer field with two goals, for example 5 against 5. Each team consists of three soccer defenders and two soccer strikers, who are only allowed to stay in one half of the field. After a certain time or after a shot on goal, the coach calls out "black out and gray in". One team should now leave the field in a flash and the gray team should take their place. After a relatively short time, the white and black teams change, and so on.

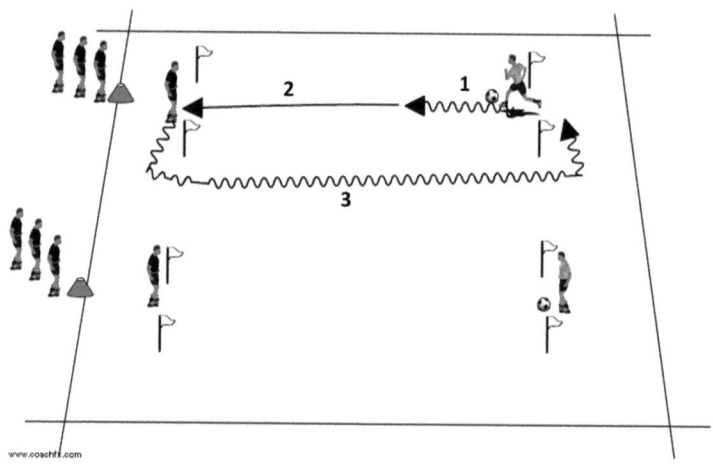

www.coachfx.com

Technique exercise

Exercise structure: see picture above

Procedure: A child with a ball stands opposite the other children at a distance of about 20 meters. The child with the ball starts, dribbles a few meters and shoots through the flagpoles to the first child in the row and stands in the back. The first child in line takes the ball and dribbles at high speed to the start and the exercise begins again.

Literaturverzeichnis

Claßen, M. / Schnepper, W.:
Taktiktraining im Jugendfußball, BOD, 2011

Claßen, M. / Schnepper, W.:
Taktiktraining im Jugendfußball 2, BOD, 2012

Claßen, M. / Schnepper, W.:
Pressing mit System, BOD, 2012Claßen, M. / Schnepper, W.:

Schnepper, W. / Claßen, M.
E-Jugend / D-Jugendtraining: effektive Übungen,
BOD, 2014

Schnepper, W. / Claßen, M.
D-Jugend / C-Jugendtraining:
30 komplette Trainingseinheiten,
BOD, 2016

Schnepper, W. / Claßen, M.
D-Jugend / C-Jugend:
über 100 effektive Trainingsübungen
BOD, 2017

Schnepper,W: Psyche im Kinderfußball, BOD, 2019

 **Notizen**